ADVENTURE TIME™

VOLUME 8

ADVENTURE TIME Volume Eight, March 2016. Published by Titan Comics, a division of Titan Publishing Group Ltd., 144 Southwark St., London, SE1 0UP. Contains material originally published in single comic form as ADVENTURE TIME No 35-39. © Cartoon Network (S16) All rights reserved. ADVENTURE TIME, CARTOON NETWORK, the logos, and all related characters and elements are trademarks of and © Cartoon Network. All characters, events and institutions depicted herein are fictional. Any similarity between any of the names, characters, persons, events and/or institutions in this publication to actual names, characters, and persons, whether living or dead and/or institutions are unintended and purely coincidental. TCM 1646

A CIP catalogue record for this title is available from the British Library.

Printed in China.

10 9 8 7 6 5 4 3 2 1

ISBN: 9781785852923
www.titan-comics.com

CREATED BY
Pendleton Ward

ISSUE 35
WRITTEN BY
Ryan North

ILLUSTRATED BY
Shelli Paroline & Braden Lamb

ISSUES 36-39
WRITTEN BY
Christopher Hastings

ILLUSTRATED BY
Zachary Sterling

COLOURS BY
Maarta Laiho

LETTERS BY
Steve Wands

COVER BY
Shelli Paroline & Braden Lamb

With special thanks to
Whitney Leopard, Shannon Watters, Marisa Marionakis, Rick Blanco,
Nicole Rivera, Conrad Montgomery, Meghan Bradley, Curtis Lelash and
the wonderful folks at Cartoon Network.

Look Marceline: a bee!

Uh...huh?

Well, this has been truly amazing and all, but I feel like maybe I'd better just go home and--

Wait wait wait! Marceline! Now there's a **BUTTERFLY!!**

And now there's a ladybug! A **LADYBUG**, Marceline!

Wait, the ladybug crawled away and now there's a worm!

Wait, the worm crawled away and now there's a **NEW** butterfly!!

They're **TOTALLY** wandering through the forest, doing so as they please! **NICE!!**

So what do you think, Marcy? Can you capture this adventure in song??

I mean, I **THOUGHT** I'd be writing a song about you guys shredding monster bosses, but yeah, sure, a song about bees and ladybugs **QUIETLY WANDERING THROUGH GRASS** is probably equally as punk.

A promise is a promise, Marcy!

Hey, can I at least throw in some electric guitar and a killer bass?

NOPE

It's a JEWEL, you guys! And somebody STOLE IT, probably to buy some stupid garbage like GROSS WHEAT or CORN!!

Stay right there, LSP. We're on our way down.

Yeah!!

Wait, why are we talking smack about corn??

Because it's gross AND nasty AND gross-nasty? But that's not important right now! MY STAR IS STOLEN!!

Is someone throwing shade on corn??

Lumpy Space Princess says she doesn't like delicious corn!

Oh my GLOB, everyone stop talking about corn and come outside and help me!!

Alright alright, calm DOWN, LSP.

Your heroes are on their way, m'lady!!

Hey, have you ever tried it with a nice slab of butter on top? DELICIOUS.

CORN'S GROSS AND YOU ACTUALLY JUST LIKE BUTTER, ICE KING!!

OPEN YOUR EYES!

Alright, LSP, tell us everything you know about what happened.

Yeah! The more we know, the better we'll be able to track down the thief!

Nice try, friendos! But I know the first rule of investigating crimes:

Don't give away any prime information...TO YOUR PRIME SUSPECTS.

Suspects? What?

That's right, Marceline! Y'ALL ARE TIED AS MY #1 SUSPECTS!!

DRAAAAMA BOMB!

LSP, we wouldn't steal your star! We peeps are WAY good-aligned!

Yeah!

I mean... generally.

Save it, chumps! I know it was one of you, and I hope y'all have some RAD ALIBIS because y'all are getting QUESTIONED on the ASAP!!

Come on, LSP. I don't even want your star. Besides, my alibi is AIR-TIGHT.

Yeah! And MY alibi is air-tighter, LSP!!

MY ALIBI IS I WAS PARTYING

Alright, "BMO", if that **IS** your real name--

It is! Yaaaay!

Why don't you tell me **EXACTLY** where you were during the night of the theft?

Okay! I love telling stories!!

BMO's ALIBI

"It was a dark and stormy night. The kind of night that made you think someone might be out there doing a crime in it somewhere."

What's this? An invitation??

Princess Bubblegum cordially invites BMO to attend her SECRET PRINCESS MEETING after which Light Refreshments will be served. TELL NO ONE

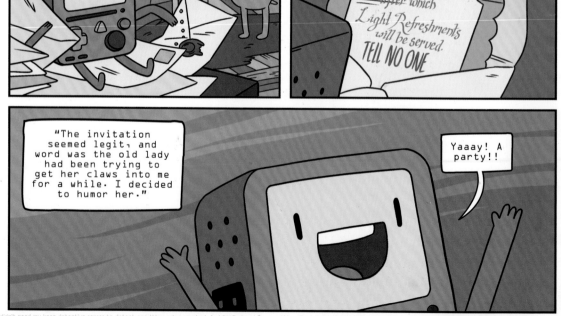

"The invitation seemed legit, and word was the old lady had been trying to get her claws into me for a while. I decided to humor her."

Yaaay! A party!!

I didn't need my keen detective senses to detect one thing: crime was bad. And BMO stood for one thing: "Best Detective, Yo." Hey, I said I was good at detection. Never said I was good at acronyms.

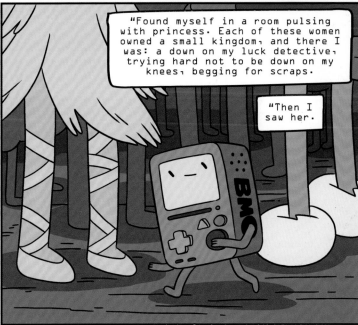

She was sweet as candy, sure, but she could be hard like hard candy and sour like sour candy too. She was metaphorically like candy in a whole kingdom's worth of ways.

"Struck me as an odd way to describe the weather. Probably would've struck me a few other ways too, but at that point someone started letting their size nines do the talking. All over my face."

Hey! Ow!!

Aw! I'm sorry, little guy!

It's okay! I'm made of metal!!

"It was an obvious distraction, but I swallowed it hook, line, and sinker...and the rest of the fishing rod too. Coulda opened a tackle shop with what I swallowed that night. Almost did."

"Truth was, she was a princess with a mouth full of teeth that didn't quit."

I don't think we've met. I'm Lamprey Princess!

I'm BMO and I like you already!!

"Maybe I let myself get distracted."

Yaaay! FRIENDSHIP!!

"She hugged me tight. Too tight. Couldn't tell you for sure what I heard then."

"Maybe it WAS the sound of a star being pulled out of someone's lumpy space head while she wasn't looking.

"Maybe it was the sound of two hearts finding each other.

"Or maybe it was just the sound of one heart fooling itself."

"All I can say for sure is she didn't do it. She had the perfect alibi: me. And I had her...for as long as it lasted."

Okay well I have to go now! Bye!!

Nice meeting you, BMO!

"Haven't seen her since that night. Tried to find her. Tried harder to forget her.

"Neither's worked."

Parties are fun and cool, just like me!!

Oh, you want to talk about whose star is hotter? Um is 15 MILLION DEGREES CELSIUS hot enough for you??

"Alright LSP, here's my alibi: I'd called an Every Princess meeting, phoning up all the princesses in Ooo. I had a proposition for them."

Attention, everyone: I have a proposition for you!

"We'd had more than our share of invasions, attacks, and jerks getting all up in our fries. What I wanted to propose was an **ADVENTURER AND HERO SHARING ARRANGEMENT**, wherein kingdoms would pool their adventurer resources, to be directed towards the greatest need for the greatest good."

In conclusion, my proposition is that thing I just said!

"My proposal was a reasonable solution to a shared problem that worked to achieve mutual benefit. As such, it was no surprise when it was accepted quickly."

PB has proposed a reasonable solution.

I concur.

"They applauded my initiative, and there were no other incidents that evening worth noting."

The next morning I met up with Finn and Jake and Marceline for breakfast as planned, and then you came running towards us, and you know the rest!

Oh my glob, I wasn't even in your alibi!

YOU EDITED ME OUT FROM YOUR OWN MEMORIES??

And so, my fellow Ooo-ians: ask not why there are jerks all up in our fries, ask why we're leaving our fries out in the first place.

You were there?

YES I WAS THERE. You said yourself it was an EVERY PRINCESS meeting! I'M A PRINCESS OF THE LUMPIEST POSSIBLE SPACE.

Obviously I was there!!

...Huh.

WAS LSP HERE?

MAYBE HERE?

WAIT, WAS THIS ACTUALLY LSP??

WAS THIS STAR ACTUALLY HERE, OR A GROSS HOLE, OR...?

Yeah, I mean, I guess you could've been there? I think I maybe remember that.

Do you even remember what you had for breakfast??

YES, LSP, I do. And before you ask: it's classified.

Anyway, that's what happened last night. Ask anyone else; they'll corroborate.

Oh, I will. I am. I am literally doing that right away, "Princess" "Bubblegum".

NEXT!!

Hey Finn, hey Jake. Thanks for coming. I'm sorry that this whole situation is so intense and dramatic.

S'cool.

Being involved in investigations is fun!!

Okay, so tell me your **EXACT** whereabouts during the night in question.

No problem! We remember it like it was yesterday!

Because it was!

Dude! Check out the size of my banner bod!

I know, it totally rules!!

FINN & JAKE'S ALIBI

"We'd heard of PB's event, so we were preparing..."

READY, Jake?

READY, Finn

WHAT TIME IS IT??

Sneaking into the princess-only meeting as **UNSOLICITED SECRET UNDERCOVER SECURITY** time!!

Even a broken clock is right twice a day!

"Getting in was no problem, thanks to our rad disguises!"

Pleased to meet you. I'm Princess Dogbod and this is my associate, Princess Cool Bear Hat. As you're probably noticing, yes, we **ARE** real princesses and not actually two dudes in disguise.

Hello.

Alright Jake. Keep an eye out for any bad guys trying to infiltrate here. Their disguises may somehow be **EVEN BETTER** than our own.

On it.

Hey guys I have something to talk about but it's gonna be hecka irrelevant, so don't feel bad if you forget what I'm saying as of right...**NOW.**

Can do, PB!

Hey! Looking good, LSP!

THANK YOU, mysterious stranger! My dress matches the star I have crammed into my head. You know the one? This star right here?

Yep! This is us observing that you definitely have the star at the start of this evening's festivities!

And this is me observing an uninvited guest stealing the whole dang snacks table!!

Gasp!

THAT'S EXACTLY WHAT A BAD GUY WOULD DO!!

YOU GUYS, yours is the worst alibi yet! I WAS THERE AND I DIDN'T SEE WYATT THERE AT ALL.

Man, memories are biz-onkers.

Just like Wyatt, who incidentally, I absolutely remember being there!

Good thing you're investigating, huh? Don't worry: I'm sure you'll uncover the truth eventually. Good luck, LSP!

Let us know when you're done! We'll take the culprit on a ride...TO JUSTICE.

Okay, bye!

And remember: we love justice!!

Why would skeletons even eat anyway?

FOOD LITERALLY GOES RIGHT THROUGH THEM!!

KRASH!

NEXT!!

Party God's Alibi

IT WAS A PARTY

EVERYONE PARTIED QUITE HEARTY

WE RAN OUT OF DRINKS

HAH HAH NO WE DIDN'T, I'M PARTY GOD

PARTY FOREVER

PARTY FOREVER

PARTY FOREVER

Yes thank you this was very helpful

AMOUBCCMQTWWQUUUICUCWWZKTWWQOQLIFHBHBXYTTOSQIAAGBZKJDSJSFHPFVZNHNGZOQSLSHDH

MARCELINE'S ALIBI

I'd helped PB set up the hall earlier that day, so I thought I'd drop in and see how things were going.

I'm listening...

When I got there, I saw Finn and Jake with some skeletons outside.

Wait, wait: this is the first thing that corroborates anything! Finn and Jake mentioned that too!

Oh. Cool.

Anyway it turns out they were all protesting. They wanted the princesses to sign a joint statement reclassifying grave-yards as "skeleton farms"?

No, wait. "RAD skeleton farms."

I'm sorry, but nobody gets seconds until everyone's had firsts.

But I'm hungry! Food goes right through me!!

I'D DEMONSTRATE IF YOU LET ME.

STICKS & STONES MAY BREAK MY BONES BUT PREJUDICIAL GRAVEYARD CLASSIFICATION REALLY HURTS ME!

PRI BU DU

O BON ABOUT EQUALI

ANTI-SKELE BIAS CHILLS M TO THE ONE

DID YOU MOVE TODAY? THANK YOUR SKELETON!

OH MY GLOB, WERE ANY OF YOU GUYS EVEN AT THE SAME PLACE?

REMIND ME TO NEVER ASK ANY OF YOU TO REMEMBER ANYTHING EVER

Ice King, I hover before you a broken princess. You're my last hope, and if you can't tell me something that makes sense, then I think my star actually **IS** lost...**FOREVER!!**

Ha ha, WOW, have you come to the wrong place! These stanky old wizard eyes aren't good for that sort of thing at all!

mek

"Listen: I'd heard about Bubblegum's party and I figured I should crash it. It sounded like a cool place to meet babes, you know?"

Hey, anyone here want to meet a lonely man??

"But I got kicked out in like five seconds."

Oh my glob get **OUT** of here, Ice King! This is a babes-only zone!!

But **I'M** a #1 babe!

You believe me when I say that, right?

Aha! So you were **SO UPSET** from my **AWESOME RULES ENFORCEMENT** that you came back that very night to steal from me??

mek

What? No! No, I went home and wrote in my diary until it was time for bed!

You want to read it? It mentions your star! I'll prove it!

DATING
ON THIN ICE

THE SEMI-FICTIONALIZED DIARY OF ONE MAN WHOSE EMOTIONS WERE ALL TOO REAL

"As LSP kicked me out, the star on her head seemed to symbolize how, much like the actual stars themselves, like the ones in space I mean, these smokin' hot megababes were destined to remain forever beyond my reach.

PASS

Hey, are you sure your star didn't just, you know...**FALL OUT** somewhere?

Well it never fell out before, Ice King!

I don't know. I thought it had to be one of you guys since you were the only ones who left before I noticed my star was missing, but now...I don't know **ANYTHING** anymore. I guess...I guess it's really gone, huh?

And now I'll never see it again and have to wear this stupid patch forever and it's not even that hot.

LSP, I know a thing or two about loss, and you know what I've learned?

Sometimes all you can do is tell yourself that losing it was the best thing that could've happened to you, over and over and **OVER** again until you finally, **FINALLY**, believe it.

UM HELLO ICE KING THAT'S THE WORST ADVICE EVER!!

mek

I'm **OUT OF HERE**, loser criminal best friends!!

I'ma find my star on my own, and I don't need **ANY** of you jerks!!

LATER:

Nope.

LATER:

Nope.

LATER:

USED HEAD GEMS

PERFECT FOR PUTTING IN YOUR HEAD

EMPTY EARHOLES? VACANT NOSEHOLES? CAVERNOUS MOUTH HOLES? PUT A GEM IN IT!

LATER:

sigh

MUCH LATER:

Everything is stupid and I hate everyone.

Hey, LSP. Wake up!

Huh?

We couldn't find your old star either, so we made you a new one!

We all pitched in with different substances!

Do you like it?

AHHHHH!

I LOVE IT I LOVE IT I LOVE IT!!

And you all made it for me together?!

Yep!

AHHH, IT'S TOO PERFECT!! THIS MEANS THERE'S GONNA BE A PART OF Y'ALL THAT'S INSIDE ME FOREVER!!

You guys are the best ever and EVERYTHING RULES AND I LOVE EVERYONE!!

YOU KNOW, NORMALLY IN THESE HAPPY ENDING SITUATIONS I SUGGEST A LITTLE SOMETHING THAT START WITH "PAR"

AND ENDS WITH "TY"

AND IS THE WORD "PARTY" WHEN YOU BRING THE TWO HALVES TOGETHER

Oh my glob, Party God...

...I THOUGHT YOU'D NEVER ASK.

MEANWHILE BACK IN Ooo:

hrm don't know why nobody else has done it mrhmble

blerh just had to **BRING IN SOME FRESH INGREDIENTS HA HA** funny but true, mbmble

hrm hrm finally going to give **OOO** it's **JUST DESSERTS**, ha ha yes... mhmm

Lorem ipsum dolor sit amet **CONSECTETUR ADIPISCING ELIT!**

WOOWMMMM

Too bad this will fling the moon into deep space.

I'll miss the moon, a mumble

But you know, not enough to stop this occult ritual that isn't ominous AT ALL.

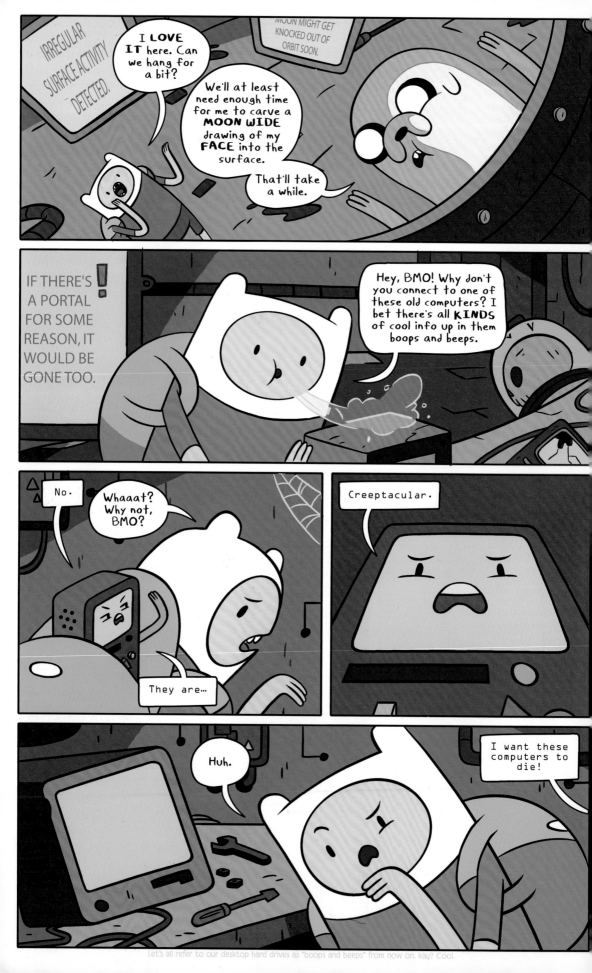

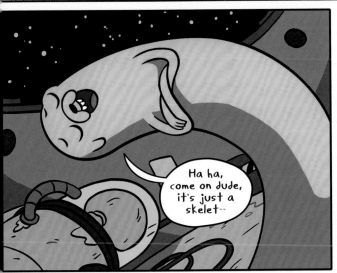

We must destroy him.

He is so evil.

EARIER TODAY...

Much training, sacrifice, and honor went into this sandwich.

And I share it with you, dear friend.

I will respect the memory of this sandwich, and your commitment to it.

In my tum tum.

CLANK!

Ha ha! Possessed your sandwich. Can't eat it now!

YOU'RE THE DEEVVVIIILLL!

They found the remains of the possessed sandwich but it's... TOO painful to show you, dear reader.

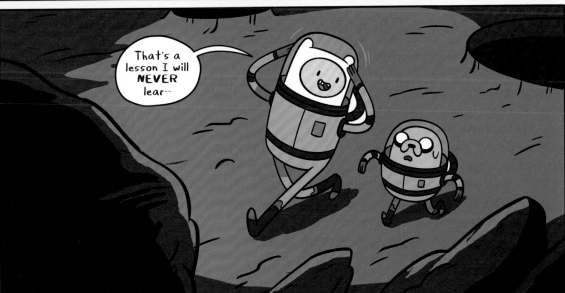

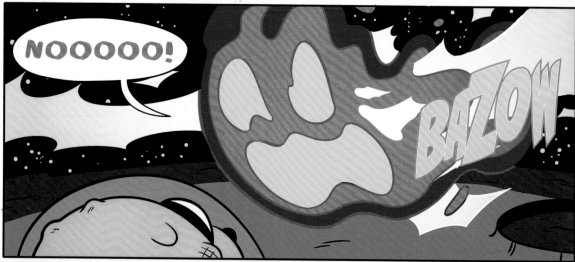

Ha ha ha

MEANWHILE:

I don't know...

...how to bake a PIE!

NO.

I saw what you said! The moon didn't go anywhere. You are a LIAR!

Let's go home, man. Give that sandwich a proper burial.

Dunk.

AH ya got me.

You're totally in the mood for a sandwich and some pie now, aren't you?

An existential crisis, probably.

I have to get to the bottom of this before **ALL THAT** happens.

Be calm, Princess.

"Be calm?" What are you, 29?

I can observe that nobody has noticed the larger implications yet.

Hey everybody! I think we **ALL FORGOT HOW TO MAKE FOOD!**

I **NEED** food! I need it to live!

HEY! I do too!

MY FEAR IS OVERIDING MY RATION-ALITY!!!

I'm going to my laboratory to figure this out! Guard the shops! Keep the peace!

Shouldn't the banana guard be helping out with this?

SMASH.

Shoo! Shame on you!

HEY YOU OVER THERE, don't mess with that **JERKY HUT.**

FANK YOU FINN, YOU FSAVED USF.

Aw jeeze, no! You have to ration that!

NUH UH.

TERROR DONUT.

Mr. Cupcake, these were for a dinner party later this week! I invited you!

GLOB KNOWS I AM NOT PROUD.

If everybody would stop panicking, we can all share what we have, and calmly come to a solution!

BRUISE

NOOOO! MY LAZERS!

FWOOOMM...

BOOP

It's okay! The sword still works as a sword! Come on! Help out!

IT'S NOT AS GOOD.

ARMY AT THE GATES.

The sword is clearly not as good, Jake.

An ARMY?!

OPEN THE GATES! LEMONGRAB FORGOT HOW TO MAKE FOOD SO YOU HAVE TO DO IT FOR US.

OR PERISH.

Sniff, I guess other people can't do food too.

No surprise Lemongrab marched his way down here. Guy's a patoot.

OH!

Oh it's everybody.

Aw, what the heck?

And why is everyone HERE? Why not raid the breakfast kingdom?

It's lunch time!

Ya lose sight of one meal, and you all turn into savages?!

Gosh, already? Oh, yeah, I guess so.

People of Ooo, hear me!

This oughta be good.

Probably doesn't want us to take all her food. HMF.

Here, ME.

I know you're scared and need to take care of your people!

I TOTALLY get that! I run at a base stress level of like A SEVEN.

I'M STRESSED TO EIGHT! NO. NINE!

MORE THAN YOU!

There is no need to raid the candy kingdom! I've found out why nobody knows how to make food, and the cure should be finished in my lab shortly!

Just... cool it outside, and we'll take care of you soon!

Wow princess, that's great.

It's a LIIIIIIIIIEEEE

All she had time to do was put on an authoritative lab coat.

I got nothin' so far. Everyone inside the candy kingdom has pretty much eaten everything. There's **MULTIPLE** armies that will only wait a little longer.

Yeah, jeeze I think every ruler in Ooo has an army out there.

Except one.

THE ICE KINGDOM:

Hello?

MY MEATLOAF FOR ONE!

PUNCH!

It totally says on the box it's for two, you GLUTTON.

Gunther stop it! You're being greedy! Lead us to the freezer!

We have to follow your penguin?

I've never actually been to the freezer. I just have my little sweeties get the food for me!

Couldn't you keep food frozen in ANY part of your castle?

I think it's just around this corner!

Oh thaaaat's why Gunther didn't want anyone down here.

CHCHCTHHH

We have one just like it. Kinda.

It's...

EMPTY.

GUNTHER! Why didn't you tell me the freezer was empty!?

Okay! Nobody needs to panic! We...we can do SOMETHING!

Got a couple scraps of meat here...

Scrape the frost off these biscuits...

Got a little mustard, pickled onion...

See?! Got a perfectly respectable sandwich! There's gotta be enough little bits in here to make some more sandwiches, right?

Who freezes MUSTARD?

Chill out, man!

It's just my stomach!

Your STOMACH would have thought I was food! It would have taken ALL MY NUTRIENTS.

I like having those nutrients around, man.

No way. I'd be all "Hey body! Don't digest Finn. He's cool!"

Found him! Looks like you zapped Finn into my tummy zone.

Ah! I specifically wanted to avoid hazards like your digestive tract!

Sorry, Finn! I tried to complete the miniaturization teleport near the source of Jake's sandwich magic and uh...

I guess if it was just going to send you to his stomach we could have just shrunk you out here and had Jake eat you.

Ha ha! Frontier science!

Ha.

"I'm Princess Bubblegum and I got excited about EXPERIMENTS and didn't think this through! Sorry!"

That's basically what she's saying.

Ha ha! Sounds right!

Jake: Good on faces. Bad on words.

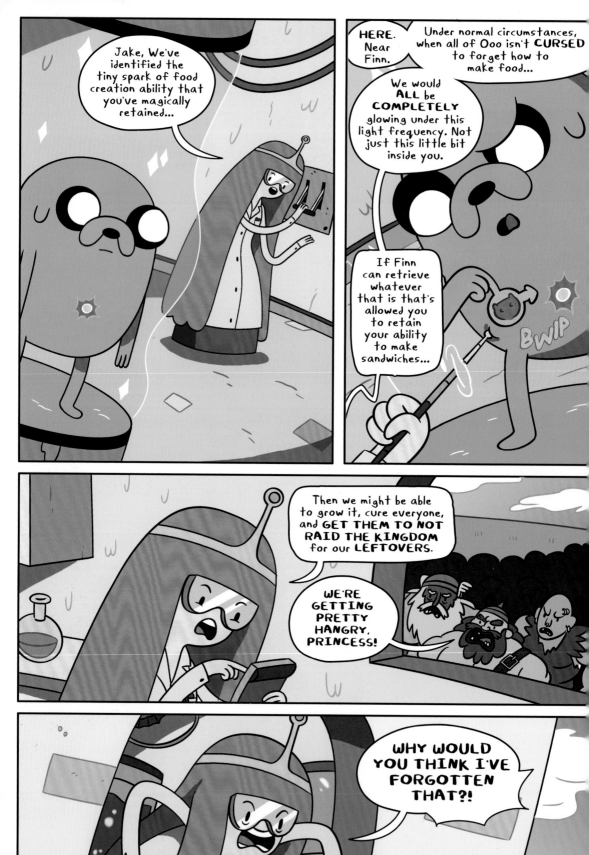

Jake, We've identified the tiny spark of food creation ability that you've magically retained...

HERE. Near. Finn.

Under normal circumstances, when all of Ooo isn't CURSED to forget how to make food...

We would ALL be COMPLETELY glowing under this light frequency. Not just this little bit inside you.

If Finn can retrieve whatever that is that's allowed you to retain your ability to make sandwiches...

BWIP

Then we might be able to grow it, cure everyone, and GET THEM TO NOT RAID THE KINGDOM for our LEFTOVERS.

WE'RE GETTING PRETTY HANGRY, PRINCESS!

WHY WOULD YOU THINK I'VE FORGOTTEN THAT?!

"Hangry" is a mix of "Angry" and "Hungry" but deep down inside, you knew that.

Don't worry, Princess! Me and Finn are **ON THE MOVE.**

Now, I must **FOCUS** on my avatar with Finn. Excuse me.

POP

Never been in **THIS** part of my body before.

What do you mean **THIS** part?

Eh, haven't been in **MOST** of it really.

Uh oh.

Invader!

That looks like immune system stuff.

Destroy invader! Protect the host!

Hey man! Don't destroy Finn. He's cool.

PROTECT THE HOST!

I AM the host you dummies! Host says he's cool!

Eeeee!

OW! Aaaaah, DUDE!

These are PART OF ME. Don't shoot lazers at ME!

ZZAAPP

But they'll... Take my health...

My sword won't work...

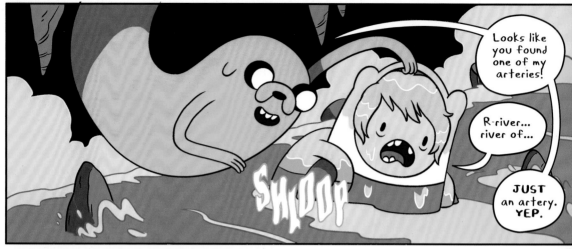

Uh, hey there guy.

Who are **YOU?**

What? I'm **JAKE.** You know who I am!

I don't.

I'm like... **ALL AROUND YOU, MAN!** I'm your king or something!

Look! I can change stuff with **MY WILL.**

hhhhhh

ARRRGHHHHH

POP

Ah!

It **IS** you! The **EATER.**

YEAH, that's right, baby--wait the what now?

Ah, welcome! The eater! The one who sent us... **THE CRYSTAL OF PERFECT SANDWICH!**

THAT WHICH CREATED US!

I think that's what we were looking for, buddy!

A perfectly preserved... tiny piece...

Of the greatest sandwich I **EVER HAD.** I remember that sandwich!

It must have gotten stuck like that! And gave me **POWERS.**

Looks like it made part of you into a **PRETTY CUTE** princess too, buddy.

Hee hee hee

What?! Oh jeeze! YOU **TWO WOULD BE PERFECT TOGETHER!**

She's a little of **ME,** your best friend! And she's a little of **SANDWICH,** the best food!

And she's **TOTAL PRIN- CESS.**

You'd have to stay in here. She can't leave.

I'd miss you, but I can come visit! I--

Dude. Chill. I don't want to go out with **ANY** princesses right now.

My sword lazers only work if I have perfect health!

Don't wanna risk a **BROKEN HEART.**

Seriously? Maybe we talk about that sword later.

What are you talking about?

Is it sandwiches?

Well, whatever you were talking about, it was with your mouths, which is where sandwiches go, so I'll just assume it was about sandwiches.

GRAAH!

I'm sorry Jake... LAZER SWORD COME TO ME.

♪ We have got a problem, girl ♪ You be chasin' me ♪ But I'll stop this squabble, girl ♪ With these lazers, see?

AAAAA MY GUTS!

Now's our chance! Smash stuff until food comes out!

WHAT?! There's no--

THERE'S NO FOOD IN ANY OF THIS!

Feel the burps. Believe in the burps.

YUSS!

BUUUURRRRRPPP

Princess! I'm out! Size me back up!

I think I heard a tiny Finn!

Seems likely, given the circumstances!

GASP!

That... gem...

If... that piece... combines with that piece...

And then it has... that condiment...

That texture... juxtaposed with **THAT** texture.

Then... that could work... **WITH ANYTHING!**

I REMEMBER HOW TO MAKE FOOD!

I hope you remember how to chew it too, because this thing shows JAKE FORGETS SOMETIMES.

I have to **SHOW EVERYONE.**

You used your sword lazers inside my guts! You **REALLY HURT ME.**

What?! Dude, those sandwich people turned into **MONSTERS.** I had to!

Plus it made you burp me out.

CLACK

I TOLD YOU, I wouldn't let any of my body hurt you!

You weren't there! You couldn't stop them!

Be honest! You just wanted to use the **SWORD LAZERS** you love so much!

That sword is **CHANGING YOU.**

YOU be honest! Part of you **DEEP DOWN** didn't want to give up your sandwich powers, and it **ATTACKED ME.**

I... remember how to make food!

It all makes sense!

That crystalized hunk of sandwich is giving me some ideas!

Let's celebrate!

A **FEAST!** Let's have A **FEAST!**

NO. You just tried to **RANSACK** my kingdom, and now you expect me to **HOST A PARTY?**

GET LOST.

We can all talk on Monday.

Here, you two. You haven't eaten either. It's okay to be cranky. Good work.

FWOOMPH

FWOOMPH

RECONCILE TIME

Sorry a hidden part deep within me wanted to destroy you!

Sorry I sword lazered you!

ELSEWHERE:

What are you doing!? You'll spoil your appetites! ARKLOTHAC IS COMING!

He's going to COOK ALL OF OOO FOR YOU TO EAT!

boo hoo

yay!

Hee hee that's better.

Don't shop for groceries hungry. Don't argue hungry. Don't rally your kingdom to go raid another kingdom hungry... There's a lesson here.

NO!

You'll spoil your appetites!

ARKLOTHAC IS COMING a herm!

Erm yes, hello! Janice Bizzle-Thatcher.

I summoned you, yes. Found a book on you and did it.

I love Ooo **SO MUCH**, and I wanted a **GREAT CHEF** who could **APPRECIATE IT** to USE the land to make the good people a **WONDERFUL MEAL** a hem, glad you're here to do it.

This world is fine. I will chop, sweat, puree, broil, and **USE** every bit of it.

And I will serve it to my ancient friends, the

I have no idea who you are.

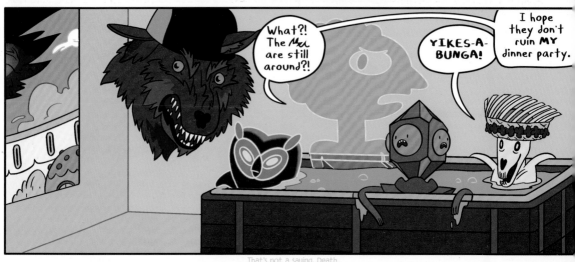

What?! The ~~are~~ still around?!

YIKES-A-BUNGA!

I hope they don't ruin **MY** dinner party.

Lady, how do we send this guy back?!

Harrum, shut down his temple?

Where's **THAT?**

There's a bunch of friendly looking reaper statues, and some crystals... and a moon symbol here or there.

'Sides! You know if one hurt me, that's it for these *HRNK* sweet lazers!

I know that place!

I thought it was an ancient outhouse.

See? Cause of the moons?

Jake, did you do good boys here?

MAYBE!

SMASH BREAK

It ain't workin' man. Dude is summoned, and ain't gettin' un-summoned.

We're just gonna have to go in, take out his little dudes, climb up the big guy, knock him around until he decides to get outta town.

You know... this dungeon reminds me a lot of...

The one on the moon!

Maybe they're connected!

I bet there's an answer there on how to use my sword lazers to beat up the big guy!

Look at the shapes, man! **MOONS!** Janice said her first try at the summoning would have knocked the moon out of orbit!

Which **MEANS** it's **IMPORTANT** and it's **CONNECTED TO MY SWORD.**

Uh...

I think you're afraid of fighting little guys who might hurt you, which will stop your sword from working.

NO!

You just want to go to the moon where you can shoot lazers at Arklothac for as long as you like without worrying about getting hit back.

That stupid sword has changed you, man. I'm gonna go fight bad guys. I'll see you when you're ready to do that again.

I AM fighting bad guys!

I'M FIGHTING SMART!

NOT FIGHTING HARD!

That's something a **BUSINESS** guy would say.

BUSINESS GUYS ARE COOL AND ADULT.

JUST LIKE RANGED FIGHTERS.

LIKE ME.

I'm just picturing an elf archer, kick-flipping on a calculator skateboard, saying "BUDGETS ARE DOPE"

First course. A consommé of water-life.

Clarified through the very clouds.

Weather today is... NOT GREAT!

The seas are boiling! The evaporated steam is quickly converting into scalding hot soup rain!

Stay inside probably.

Almost to the moon portal! And you know what?

It doesn't hurt! You hear me, sword?! IT DOESN'T HURT!

NICE DAY FOR A STROLL THROUGH SOME SOUP!!

I LOVE IT!

TSSSSSSS

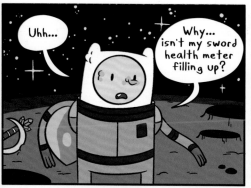

Uhh...

Why... isn't my sword health meter filling up?

BOO, BOO KISS

BOO BOO KISS

It's **NOT WORKING!**

Beemo will kiss your boo boos, Finn!

Sorry, Beemo. Robot lips don't have enough healing love power in them for something **THIS** bad...

Just like mine I guess.

Oh.

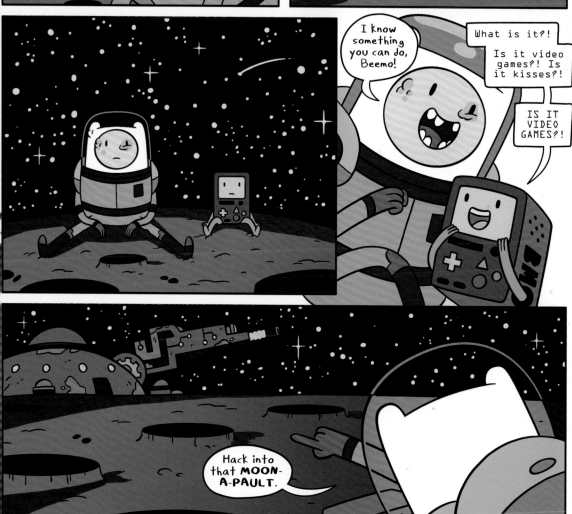

I know something you can do, Beemo!

What is it?! Is it video games?! Is it kisses?!

IS IT VIDEO GAMES?!

Hack into that **MOON-A-PAULT.**

It's... kind of video games.

Holy dimension hole, man.

Sorry I lost trust in you. Clearly you are still mega heroic.

That fall would have been... uh... pretty bad.

Nah, it was a good call. I was being weird.

THE THRILL OF A SPACE MELEE ATTACK SHOWED ME THAT.

Anyway, I knew you'd catch me!

What if I just thought you were a meteorite, man.

I'm not in the habit of running and catching all the meteorites I see.

Yikes-a-bunga.

THE END!

Jeeze, now that monster's gonna possess a submarine or something.

COVER GALLERY

Issue 35B Cover:
Mychal Amann

Issue 35C Cover:
Jimmy Giegerich

Issue 36 Cover:
Justin Hillgrove

Issue 36 Subscription Cover:
Ale Giorgini

Issue 36 Variant Cover:
Rebekka Dunlap

Issue 36 Comics Pro Variant Cover:
Sean Chen
with colors by Whitney Cogar

Issue 37 Subscription Cover:
Jerry Gaylord

Issue 37 Variant Cover:
Justin Hillgrove

CAPSULE

¥100 コイン投入口↘

Issue 38 Cover:
George Bletsis

Issue 38 Variant Cover:
Zé Burnay

Issue 39 Cover:
George Bletsis